Dead Reckoning
Poems

by Gene Auprey

POETS WEAR PRADA • HOBOKEN, NJ

DEAD RECKONING

First North American Publication 2010.

Copyright © 2010 Gene Auprey

All rights reserved. Except for use in any review or for educational purposes, the reproduction or utilization of this work in whole or in part in any form by electronic, mechanical or other means, now known or hereafter invented, including xerography, photocopying and recording, or in any informational or retrieval system, is forbidden without the written permission of the publisher. Poets Wear Prada, 533 Bloomfield Street, Second Floor, Hoboken, New Jersey 07030.

Grateful acknowledgment is made to the following publications where some of these poems have previously appeared or will soon appear:

Bird's Eye reView, *The Flea*, *Hawk & Whippoorwill*, *Lucid Rhythms*, *Oak Bend Review*, *Other Poetry*, *Pisgah Review*, *The Shit Creek Review*, *Soundzine*, and the print anthology *Poems of Inspiration and Faith* (Level 4 Press, 2009).

ISBN 978-0-9841844-5-3

Library of Congress Control Number: 2010905635

Printed in the U.S.A.

Cover Art: "Midnight Blue," photo, 2009, Esmahan Özkan

Author Photo: Sarah Merrill

Illustration: "Winter Gaiety," monotype, 1942, Seth Hoffman; private collection of the publisher *for Raylene*

Contents

Heights Attained	1
Sheltered	2
Chores	3
Child's Play (1963)	5
Devout	7
First Crop	8
Cracks	9
Blessed	10
The Wentworth Hotel, Woodsville, 1967	11
Winter Fare	12
Fear of Heights	13
Lost	14
Summer Sun	15
Counting Sheep	16
An Apology	17
Table Talk	18
Stifled	19
The War Between Us	20
Trap Line Projection	21
Apex	22
Legacy	23
roadside spring	24
Memorial Baskets	25
Cart-Right	26
Hell (descending)	27
A Woodsman's Lament	28
An Echo Affair	29

Happenstance	30
Down Slope	31
To Death	32
Hypoxia's Ghosts	33
Hospice	34
Resurrection	35

Winter Gaiety

Epilogue – The Good Life

Acknowledgments

About the Author

About the Cover Artist

About the Illustrator

*Mediocrity is the measured space
a man fills before he dies.
I used to chisel granite;
now I whittle pine.*

Heights Attained

Juniper crowds the summit trail,
scratches at a hiker's unclad legs.
Root-laced soil clings to ledge,
supports the stunted fir where fool hens
come to roost and seekers crane their necks
to watch the raven's thermal glide —
hear its throaty croak mock
the tree line bound. Mystics
call this spiritual but if one climbs
above, there is only wind and rock.

Sheltered

The farmstead's fading footprints
pocked the land of Grover Stone.
Tumbled rocks and maple trees
have claimed the cellar holes.
I measured each depression
against the stories Mother told:
of canning scalds and burning barns,
children with the grippe—a breech
turned by a midwife and frozen
chamberpots. The land slopes
toward the river and the house
where I was born, sheltered
from those hardships that made
my mother strong. I'd come to dig
for bottles in a dump she'd said
was there, buried now by fifty years
of leaves mulched black as death.
I left with just some lilacs that
still bloomed by the old well,
hoping that their scent might linger
longer in the lee of Grover's hill.

Chores

It all happened the winter I was four.
Dad allowed I'd coasted long enough;
it was time I had a steady chore.
He pointed to the black cook stove,
said; "Boy, you keep that wood box full,
that will be enough for now."
Well, biscuit wood is light, so I
could fill it in two trips
from our old woodshed.
But I protested just the same,
"I would rather fetch the eggs."
Dad, not one to take things back,
puffed hard on his hand-rolled cigarette.
The paper burst to flame. He pinched it,
coughed, "Ya know that's your sister's job."
"Then let me milk the goats," I said,
moving out of reach. He got real quiet,
pushed his hat up with one hand;
the other bid me come. Reluctantly
I did. He sat me on his lap,
put that old hat down on my head.
"What the matter boy? I know
how much you hate them goats."
Figured I been had, so I might as well come clean;
"Lina said there's witches in the shed."
I told how she brought me there
the other night, made me listen at the door,
and how things inside were banging,
clanging – all sorts of scary noise.
"She said that they were rolling bones
of little boys who pulled their sister's hair."
He laughed. "I heard 'em Dad and they were big."
"There ain't no witches son, them is just plain ol' river rats

come in to spend the winter warm." He put me down
and stood to leave, now he'd set me straight.
But I tugged his pants so he would stoop,
"I could always feed the pig."

Child's Play (1963)

With our noses pinched against
the pungent smell of the river's
churn below, we vaulted the guardrail
and skidded down through briars
that scratched and clutched bare limbs.
There, we eased the burn of the mile trek
barefoot on hot tar, in the ooze of mud
that crept from water's edge
with each August drought.

We'd come to play among the skids
of stiff blue hides, stored five rows deep
along the Contoocook's bank.
They made a fitting fort from which one
could watch water tumbling, red then green,
from beneath the tannery.
Earlier, we had stopped to see
if Sam could come along,
but his mother said, "He's sick."
We thought he was just embarrassed
because he lost his hair.

Downstream, mica seeped
to an eddy in soft clouds.
The milk-white goo shimmered
on our skin as anxious fingers
sifted muck for moonstones
and foreign coins that sometimes
we found there. I had been inside
the old mill that ground the mica schist
to powder fine, which my Dad
had bagged and stacked each night
back when he could breathe.

Come noon, we waded to where
the water ran real swift; we overturned
flat rocks, found nymphs and hellgrammites,
enough to fill a rusted can, and figured,
next day we'd come to fish.

Devout

Aunt Leona, she was stout. Squished
bees with her bare thumb, so I never
called her fat. She wore slippers
hooked from bread-wrappers we saved
for her all year, so she'd make us plastic rugs.
Her favorite saint was Anthony: *the finder
of things lost*, though he never found
her tooth—left a pink spot in her smile.

My sisters didn't like her because
she called them names when they
wore their dresses short. Her daughter
Dottie Ellen drowned at seventeen, when
she swam too near the dam. My sister
Linda couldn't save her, as she never
learned to swim. We all went to
Auntie's house, knelt with her and prayed
that they would find the body soon.

Two weeks, it caught up on some rocks
before the tannery. Aunt Leona
made me say I would thank St. Anthony.

First Crop

In a hayfield tall with timothy,
the three of us had spent midday
playing games with what we had.
A turf bomb aimed had gone awry;
one girl hit the other by mistake.

Retaliation was all-out war.
They lashed with grass pulled by the roots—
wide blades that scratched and muddied
the exposed soft skin of warriors
twin-dressed in shorts and halter tops.

Dirt ran with sweat down sun-burnt thighs
as exhaustion led them to embrace.
Each sank to taste the other's tears.
They touched as if they were alone,
kneeling there on trampled green.

Embarrassed, but yet slow to leave
two girlfriends that were near fourteen,
a twelve-year-old kept what he'd seen.

Cracks

When the temperature dropped
the river ice shifted and snapped
at times as loud as a rifle shot.
Awake, I'd pull my bedding tight
to ward off both the dread and chill.
Come dawn I'd test each step I took
to check my shiner traps. I knew
the ice would hold but still, there were
those cracks: thumb-wide fissures, rent
shore to shore. White with hoarfrost,
they mapped a child's fear of things
he couldn't stop: the cold that stayed,
a father's cough that split the night,
those thoughts of being left alone.

Blessed

Rebekah cursed, between drawn knees,
the size of her first born, but God
she loved the little one, who slipped
out next, his hand held tight to brother's
heel. She always nursed the youngest
first, for the elder sucked her dry.
Her favor was cloaked until the twins
were men — when she unveiled revenge
against the brute who wrecked her womb.
She helped the second become the first,
with no remorse for her deceit;
she knew God loved the little one.

The Wentworth Hotel, Woodsville, 1967

The room was dim with yellow light against
the grease-dark cherry walls. The bar, redone
in cheap formica, was dotted by a hundred
burns. Red stools, rimmed with pitted chrome,
moaned in protest to a patron's spin. There were booths
with duct-taped benches and splay-footed tables
that, save for the matchbook shims, would tip and rock
to an elbow's weight; at one of these I slouched,
sipping coffee, while I waited for the bar to close.

It was the fall that I turned seventeen.
I had a friend who worked there nights; last call,
he'd slip a case of long necks out the back
for me to snag and stash for a later split.
We'd done the crime a dozen times before,
and any qualms I may have had were dulled
by our routine. Bored, I stared out to the night.

My coffee trembled, creeping ever closer
to the edge. The window brightened — white with light;
there, framed by an arc of black, peeling letters,
was the old train station across the way.
Its wooden posts strobed eerily to the squeal
and clank of steel on steel. Broken glass peeked
from boarded windows like eyes from another time.

Woodsville's a place of shrieks and wandering lamps
And cars that shook and rattle — and one hotel.[1]

Jarred from my thoughts by a sudden pall of dark,
I turned away; the freight still shook the room.
Paul winked. It was time for Frost and me to leave.

---

1. From "A Hundred Collars" by Robert Frost

Winter Fare

I wonder 'bout the snowshoe hare
who gnaws the bark off willow scrub
and sleeps beneath stark junipers.
Never will he go to ground, to hide
safe from his predators. He runs
but always circles back to where
first startled from his melted bed.
Perhaps he knows it's just life's lot
to feel the talons of the owl,
the swipe of bobcat claws raking
fur from hide or the fetid crunch
of fox jaws meeting 'round his neck.
His sole defense is a passive one
at which he does excel: fucking
other bunnies — until nature's plate
abounds, leaving some leftover.

Fear of Heights

Grey nimbus, pricked by pines that climb
along the alpine crest, release the rain
that dampens my descent. Five hours ago
I stared out to the west, sun warmed despite
the constant wind. You'd taken me as high
as one could hope, then seeing all that lay
between my mountain and your sea, I turned
and headed down, afraid that in a storm
I would stumble through the night.

Lost

I looked for you, when snow was fresh
and depressions left, pooled with scent,
expecting a bell-voiced hound to drive
a bobcat 'round a cedar swamp.
When beaver swam beneath black ice
to feed beds packed with poplar tops,
your snares did not impede their way.
I listened, when the moon was bright
for the mimicry of a dying hare;
searched blue shadows at forest edge
for your hunkered form. It wasn't there.

I found snowshoes, ash grey, gut lace
gnawed through by mice, behind the shed.
The dogs are gone, some dead, some sold
to pay for living beyond one's prime.

If memory holds, I'll try again
when birches bend branch to ground
to unconfound your aged back-trail.

September Sun

The low slung Merc bucked, plowed turf
that grew between the tire ruts worn
in Jordon's pasture road, which wound
its way along the river's bank.
We passed clay cliffs where swallows hunted
one last hatch before departing south.
A half mile on, we parked; the road
was blocked. A bar gap, chained and locked
meant A.J.'s yearling bulls were still turned out.
I told her there might come a time
when it would be best to run. She laughed,
said she would take that chance. We climbed
the fence, then followed a cow path
through an alder sump mucked black
by cattle treading as they drank.
Pant legs caked and stiff, we kept on
to the rivers edge; dried crawl grass crept
beneath our clothes, tickling us to run
until we hit the sand. The river bent
to form a shallow bar that rose
in dunes, far as one could see.
We stripped and waded out to ease
our itching skin. I went back to swish
the mud still clinging to our clothes
and set them out to dry. She sat, water
rippling 'round her form, head tilted
to the warm noon sun, giggling that
minnows nipped her tender parts. I knew
then I would ask that she spend her life
with me. Twelve years later, it was I
who ran to chase the setting sun.

Counting Sheep

Within the fog that ushers sleep, I find
a level spot, stack rocks to hold stout sills
squared with an adze so they won't shift or roll.
The walls I cut from Sitka spruce, then notch
the ends to interlock. The roof is cedar,
split with a froe and pegged to purlin-poles.
A stream provides the stones I set with mud
to form a fireplace. The door is white, hewn smooth
from poplar wood, and opens to my dream:
A yard grubbed clean of stump and brush, blue asters
crowd a peastone walk that ends at forest's
edge. I shade my eyes to search its length
as if my stare could marry want to need
and bring you there, walking through my night.

An Apology

In a cup, hewn from a burl of Baltic birch,
blond grain turns dark at the twist of the knot.
I would not have noticed had I kept it full
of all you gave to me: small rocks that taste
of salt and earth, the blue feather from a jay,
spring violets dried in pale bouquet to scent
my winter's night. Such things as these once filled
this simple wooden mug; empty now, it bares
my thoughtlessness and most sincere regret.

Table Talk

A .22 short behind the ear will punch
a blackened hole and make your eyes protrude
in death. My blade will part sinew from bone,
an inch above your two hind hocks, to take
the gambrel's hooks. The chatter of a chain
will be your dirge as blocks squeak in refrain.
I'll cut a vein inside your neck and let
the mess run to the floor. Then I will smoke
a cigarette before I make you meat.

So runt, because you try so hard to move
your litter mates, I thought you ought to know —
that old sow's teat is not the prize you think.

Stifled

We moved the couch onto the porch,
the TV to my sister's room. Tin chairs
now line the wall. Dad lies cold amid
the blooms arranged by Wendell Butts
in loving memory. A wicker conch hangs
on the door; it holds a small bouquet,
to sign of what's inside. Tomorrow
they will come: a town of mourners
for their own. But now the night is thick;
the scent of flowers smothers me.

The War Between Us

We hunted coon and talked of dogs
long dead, with some the better for it.
I built his barn; he fixed my truck.
We pooled spare cash to pay for bats
and balls and beer for our weekend
softball games. He'd raise two pigs,
I'd butcher both, one for his freezer
and one for mine. It went that way
in much we did, except the past
we never shared. His was mired still
in Asian mud, its leeches and biting
gnats; while mine was spared those times
by a lottery in '69.

Trap Line Projection

A mound of cattail stalks and mud rises 'round
from black ice on the slough. Five-dollar rats
are warm within its limited confines;
a small hole rimmed by hoarfrost tells me this
is true. Thin ice makes a poor window, but if
I kneel and squint, four runs come into view.
A one-ten staked in each should mean a Jackson
scored by dawn. I will pull them then, to leave
some seed, and case skin what they've caught.
The meat I'll use to bait my fisher sets,
for they're what pays the bills. I'll stow the rats,
sell them on the sly — because I'm saving up
for Valentine's Day, just two weeks away.
I'll not forget, and maybe she will stay.

Apex

The mountain's peak, all crags and stunted spruce,
twice lured me with its test of legs and wind
that pushed full gale across the granite nub.
I crawled, sore kneed, to touch a tethered flag;
whip-snapped, it bled from burgundy to rose
between the first and second time I climbed.
I no longer strive to gain a pennant's fading
worth. And heights I've gained are measured not
in feet but as the time I have to spend
with you, whose color deepens at my touch.

Legacy

Paths I have never walked
are worn black on the forest floor.
Flowers I cannot name
unfold to catch the morning sun.
The river runs its course
when I'm not there to watch it flow.
Grass turns to snow, turns to grass
growing on my father's grave.

roadside spring

tree frogs peep and preen for love
as I touch the fur of willow buds
sun warmed against the morning's chill
five branches snapped I should bring them home
to the milk glass vase still ribboned
with blue lace that tied the now dead
violets I brought for her last fall
when I thought she would be there
but water has seeped into my shoes
and the tree frog's mock wears thin
I leave them here in an old beer can
a gift in case some other lover stops
he can leave here with dry feet

Memorial Baskets

If Mom weren't dead, she'd shame me till
I split white ash and wove the shook
to hold the potted buds she'd lay
the last of May on all the graves
of our departed relatives.
But since she's gone, the flowers stay
in pots upon the window sill,
an honor to the care she took
and I remember every day.

Cart-Right

The he-horse nickered a smile,
hinds kicked to fend the whiffletree.
Chest heaved tight in the collar,
he was ready to run — or not.
Maybe he'd rear back against
the britchen, foul the trace slack
on the hames. Five-years old,
ill broke to pull, he'd run away twice
with the light show dray, stove its wheels
and an old man's ribs up some. Now,
that horse is not hooked to a flimsy cart,
but snatched to a stone sled, set
in the center of a twenty-acre field.
The man with the reins weighs
the whip in his hand, sits back on the bench,
feet braced for a turn or two. Soon —
split leather will snap near the stud's
right ear as the driver gives him his head.
The horse will run till he's sucking wind,
then the whip will crack once more.
When his legs break down he'll be walked
to the barn. Tomorrow — back to the dray.

Hell (descending)

Well, it's hot, but not from brimstone's rage;
the burn is more akin to want. There's thirst,
if one can call it that, to slake the need
of being known. The crush of souls, another
myth, they're here but never reach to touch —
demons too, from time to time, they pass
like a wisp of scent: flowers you cannot find.
The presence of eternity is something else
that isn't here. You try, but cannot speak
your name; it's gone and left you. Where?

A Woodsman's Lament

If I were a buck, with velvet worn
from spindled tines, muzzle grayed
and teeth too poor for acorn feed,
I still could scent a dark earth scrape
and search fall's wind for estrus doe.
Perhaps I'd try, in a suitor's duel,
one last clash with rut-necked youth,
and chance a death in golden leaves
within fair sight of love.

But I am not that stalwart stag
and autumn's wind blows cold.

An Echo Affair

I was laid back on paper sheets
and coated with a slippery gel to ease
the slide of a sonic mouse that probed
my bare left side, while prodded on the right
by a pretty tech's quite perk C-cup.
The doppler did what dopplers do—
a sound image of my heart, fast falling
for this girl in green, who smiled white
and smelled of lanolin. It was over all
too soon. I was given tissue, told to wipe
and put my shirt back on. Then she
was gone with the sound of my still
beating heart cradled softly in her arms.
I was left with nothing but the bill.

Happenstance

The beech hangs there, roots exposed,
cantilevered by a runnel's wash.
Fifty years of girth, grown stout,
support its wide, spread boughs.
Defiantly it buds each spring,
though summer leaves might catch
the wind and bring its height to ground.

Down Slope

The ascent was slowed by rabbit trails;
worn paths diverged then circled back.
They all converged on level ground—
flat apogee attained by those who'd yet
to hear the bawl of hounds picking up
the back trail.

                Once I heard the dogs,
one path to follow down. The way
was clear, no stone or brush to slow
the pace of my decent. Flowers passed
were mauve—fast fading to a pink—
tinged white then wilted-brown.

                      The scent
of grass, the taste of earth, grow stronger
with each step. The din behind now pulses,
pushes hard. I'll soon be run to ground.

To Death

It is funny we should be such friends
considering our start.
I cursed you when my father died,
and when Donnie's dad shot him,
thinking he was a deer.
The others didn't hurt as much;
my passion cooled by age
until the day you took my son.
Then I just wanted to be next.
Instead, you came to live with me
residing in my chest.
Each time I cough and fight for air,
I know that you are there,
holding in your hand all my memories
you've garnered one by one.

Hypoxia's Ghosts

*Their haunting is not unpleasant
and not entirely unprovoked.
Blood flow being somewhat scant
the brain prefers what's been resolved
to issues that require actions and air.*

It would rather:

Swim with Bonnie Hawks,
watch her rise like some blonde trout
and roll her white ass high to dive again.
See her twist wet hair into a knot,
as she sprawls across the slat-wood dock.

Hear the whine of Dad's bench saw
ripping pine for furniture, bind to a hum.
Jump when he yells; "Shim the cut," instead
of standing like some fool who wouldn't
"Know enough to lick salt and drool."

Run barefoot 'round slow Jersey cows,
hop the fence to John Bean's woods.
Meet Russell at Dutch Hole, an upturned stump
and place of secrets never to be told.

Hospice

The cherry is choked in brown-tail webs.
Its leaves, thirst-curled, are silent
though the wind bids them rattle;
they move in unison, encapsulated
by the silken mesh of larval worms.
There will be no tension, no violence
of torque and twist, stem wrenched
to flight. They'll not know lift
and soar as they float to oblivion;
bound, they simply wither of life.

Resurrection

What is this bog but an expanse of white
with tufts on hummocks and dead sentry ash,
where life follows channels entombed by ice?
Years past, I came with snare and axe
to rob this grave in March, before the sun
could roll aside the weight of winter's stone
and call the living forth to mate and dam the flow.
But now it's late and snow, moon-blue,
gathers in my boots and cools my blood.
I've come to ask the ash how much longer need they stand.

Winter Gaiety

Epilogue

The Good Life

Nights are the time to practice dying,
with daytime cares no longer vying
for numbered breaths and measured beats.
Relax and slip between cold sheets.
Let them evoke where you'll be lying
when medicine and you stop trying
to stay the hand of consequence.

Acknowledgments

Poems in this volume have been published or are scheduled to appear, sometimes in different versions, in the following journals and anthologies. To the editors, thanks are due.

Bird's Eye reView	"Stifled"
The Flea	"Down Slope"
Hawk & Whippoorwill	"Lost"
Lucid Rhythms	"Cracks," "Resurrection," "The War Between Us"
Oak Bend Review	"roadside spring"
Other Poetry	"Hospice"
Pisgah Review	"Heights Attained," "Winter Fare"
Poems of Inspiration and Faith, edited by William H. Roetzheim (Level 4 Press, 2009)	"Hell (descending)"
The Shit Creek Review	"Blessed"
Soundzine	"Counting Sheep," "Sheltered," "Table Talk"

Special thanks to Charles Musser and Ethan Anderson for their gracious and talented help in editing both the poems and the manuscript.

About the Author

 Gene Auprey is Senior Editorial Adviser for *Soundzine*, an online international literary journal located at http://www.soundzine.net.

His poems have appeared in *The Flea, Hawk & Whippoorwill, Lucid Rhythms, Other Poetry, Pisgah Review*, and *The Shit Creek Review,* as well as many other places, both pixel and print.

Gene currently lives in Buxton, Maine. Widely traveled and a dedicated outdoors man, he enjoys the company of his grandchildren. He has worked across the United States in construction, designed and built many homes, managed diverse companies, and also served as an ordained minister. While his poetry has many influences, perhaps the strongest has been New England's poet laureate, Robert Frost.

About the Cover Artist

Esmahan Özkan lives in Ankara, Turkey and is a fourth-year university student. While working mainly in macro, detailed and abstract photography, she is now attempting to master portrait photography, and prefers to work in black and white and sepia tones.

About the Illustrator

Seth Hoffman (1895-1948), the Philadelphia/New York artist, studied at Pennsylvania Academy of Fine Arts with Philip Hale, Emil Carlsen, Daniel Garber, C. Grafly, and H. McCarter, and at the Ecole des Beaux-Arts, Paris. Hoffman was a member of the Woodstock Artists Association and taught at I.L.G.W.U., NYC. By profession painter, etcher, and teacher, most noted for his black & white monotypes, his work was exhibited at Pepsi-Cola, 1945; National Academy of Design, 1940; solo shows: Macbeth, Grand Central, Milch Galleries, NY; Casson Gallery, Boston; O'Brien Gallery, Chicago; Tilden & Thurber Gallery, Providence; Milwaukee Art Institute; Detroit Institute of Arts; Grand Rapids Art Gallery; Westchester Center, White Plains, NY. Hoffman's monotypes can be found in the permanent collections of the Smithsonian American Art Museum, Washington D.C., and the Herbert F. Johnson Museum of Art, Cornell University, NY. (Seth Hoffman is the paternal grandfather of the editor/publisher Roxanne Hoffman.)

www.ingramcontent.com/pod-product-compliance
Lightning Source LLC
Chambersburg PA
CBHW051712090426
42736CB00013B/2666